CW00840957

# All the Good Things About TURNING 40

ISBN 978-1543054163

21484902R00061

Printed in Great Britain
by Amazon